118-11th Street East
Prince Albert, Sk S6V 1A1

A Ticket to
France

Tom Streissguth

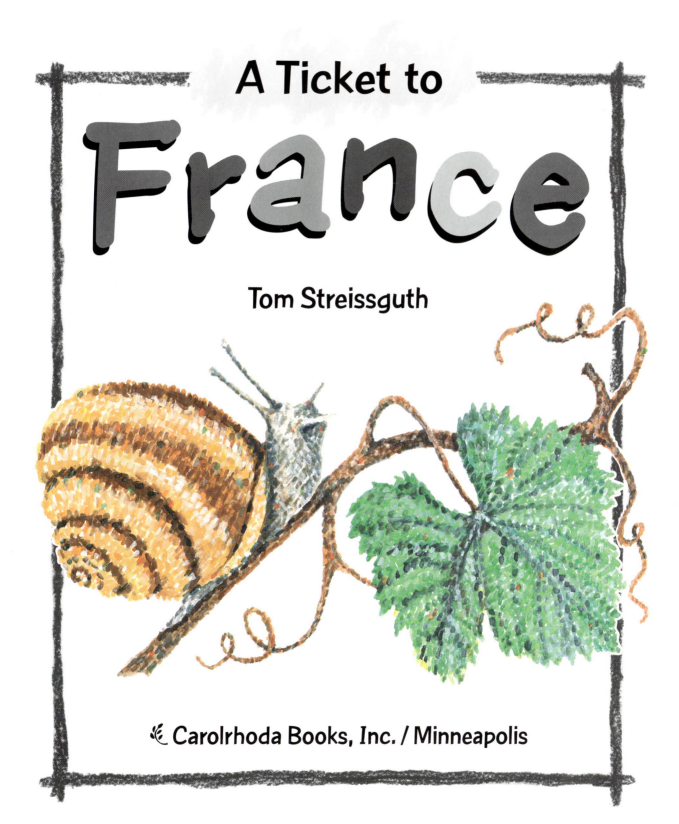

🌿 Carolrhoda Books, Inc. / Minneapolis

Photo Acknowledgments

Photographs, maps, and artworks are used courtesy of: John Erste, pp. 1, 2–3, 35, 40–41; Laura Westlund, pp. 4–5, 19, 28–29, 38–39, 45; © Robert Fried, pp. 6, 9 (right and bottom), 11, 12, 13 (left), 14, 15 (top and bottom), 17 (left and right), 18, 20 (top), 21, 22 (bottom), 23, 26 (top), 28, 30, 31 (left), 32, 33, 35, 37 (bottom); Buddy Mays/TRAVEL STOCK, pp. 7, 13 (right), 20 (bottom), 24, 27, 37 (top); © Michele Burgess, pp. 8, 10; French Government Tourist Office, pp. 9 (left), 25 (top right by Fred Slavin), 42 (bottom); © Eugene G. Schulz, pp. 13 (middle), 42 (top); © M. Kimak, pp. 16, 29; Chris Fairclough, pp. 22 (top), 31 (right), 36; Bob Wolfe, p. 25 (left); American Egg Board, p. 25 (bottom right); Burch Communications, Inc., p. 26 (bottom); A. A. M. van der Heyden, p. 34; Sportschrome, p. 38; Erich Lessing/Art Resource, NY, p. 43; Independent Picture Service, p. 44. Cover photo of French boys © Robert Fried.

Copyright © 1997 by Carolrhoda Books, Inc.

All rights reserved. International copyright secured. No part of this book may be reproduced, stored in a retrieval system, or transmitted in any form or by any means—electronic, mechanical, photocopying, recording, or otherwise—without the prior written permission of Carolrhoda Books, Inc., except for the inclusion of brief quotations in an acknowledged review.

Carolrhoda Books, Inc.
c/o The Lerner Publishing Group
241 First Avenue North
Minneapolis, Minnesota 55401 U.S.A.
Website address: www.lernerbooks.com

Library of Congress Cataloging-in-Publication Data

Streissguth, Thomas, 1958–
 France / by Tom Streissguth.
  p. cm. — (A ticket to)
 Includes index.
 Summary: Discusses the people, geography, religion, language, customs, life-styles, and culture of France.
 ISBN 1-57505-128-1 (lib. bdg. : alk. paper)
 1. France—Social life and customs—20th century—Juvenile literature.
[1. France.] I. Title. II. Series.
DC33.7.S77   1997
944.081–DC21   97-357

Manufactured in the United States of America
1 2 3 4 5 6 – JR – 02 01 00 99 98 97

Contents

Welcome!	4	Shopping	28
The Land	6	School and Summer	30
Paris	8	Faiths of France	32
Traveling	10	Let's Celebrate!	34
The French	12	Vacation	36
Newcomers	14	On Your Bikes!	38
Cities and Towns	16	Story Time	40
Sharing Words	18	Art	42
Homes	20	*New Words to Learn*	44
Family	22	*New Words to Say*	46
Food	24	*More Books to Read*	47
And More Food	26	*New Words to Find*	48

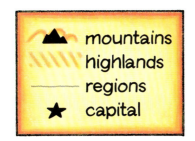

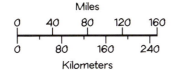

France covers a lot of the **continent** of Europe. Except for European Russia, France is the biggest country in Europe.

Three sides of France touch water and three touch land. The three bodies of water that meet France are the English Channel to the north, the Atlantic Ocean to the west, and the Mediterranean Sea to the south. The countries that touch France's other three sides are Spain, Italy, Switzerland, Germany, Luxembourg, and Belgium.

A farmhouse in the Pyrénées

The Land

Much of France's land is rolling hills. But the Alps and the Pyrénées, two high sets of **mountains,** are also in France. Massif Central means "central highland." The highland is a **plateau** that covers much of southern France. On the highland, many round black-stone mounds rise straight up from the ground.

The longest river in France is the Loire River. Workers dug **canals** in between France's biggest rivers to link them to one another. Large ships do not use these waterways anymore, but small boats float along the canals, just for fun. Toot, toot!

A farmer strolls through his grapevines in southern France.

Paris

Paris is the **capital,** or government center, of France and the largest city in the country. This big city began as a village on the Seine River. Paris spread out onto both sides of the Seine River. Life in Paris moves fast. Many

Paris spreads out from both sides of the Seine River.

travelers come just to see the city and places nearby. Paris has many famous places to visit.

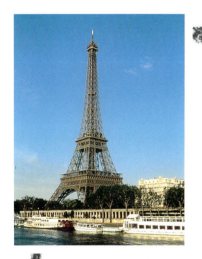

The Eiffel Tower was built in 1889 for the world's fair.

The Arc de Triomphe took 30 years to build.

A Tour of Paris

Versailles is a palace near Paris where French kings once lived.

Traveling

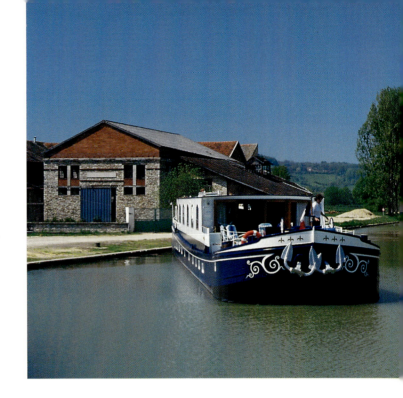

French drivers go fast on the big highways. But in small towns and villages drivers must go slowly. The roads are narrow. Two cars can barely squeeze past one another. If you need to swerve away from a truck or a cow, you might have to drive into a field!

Many people who live in cities do not own a car. If they want to go somewhere, they hop on a train. One kind of train goes at very high speeds. Whoosh!

People in France can travel on a waterway called a canal (left) or by a very fast freeway (above).

Map Whiz Quiz

Take a look at the **map** on page four. Trace the outline of France onto a piece of paper. Can you find the Atlantic Ocean? Mark this side of your map with a "W" for west. Do you see Spain? Mark it with an "S" for south. How about Switzerland? Mark this side with an "E" for east. Then look for the English Channel. Mark your map with an "N" for north. Color in the areas labeled the Alps and the Pyrénées.

Waving French teenagers

The French

Gauls, Romans, Franks, Normans, and Basques are groups of people who ruled parts of France long ago. This is part of the reason French people do not always look alike or speak exactly the same.

In the south, many French people have darker skin and hair. They might have Roman ancestors. A lot of northern French have blond hair and blue eyes. Those features may come from the Normans. The Basques still live in the southwestern corner of France.

Picnickers near the English Channel

A shopper in Provence

A fruit seller from Lyons

Newcomers

French students pile off the bus.

France used to own many lands on the continents of Asia and Africa. The French government gave the people who lived on these lands the right to move to France. The largest group of people who moved to

France is from North Africa. The reason many people have come to France is to make a better life for their families. Most newcomers speak French plus their own language.

(Top) *This bakery makes goods like those eaten in Tunisia.* (Right) *A woman originally from Morocco helps visitors at a French train station.*

Cities and Towns

Most French live in big cities. Traffic whizzes by on the streets. People bump into one another on the narrow sidewalks.

(Facing page) *Honk! Honk! Traffic jams are part of life in Paris.*

Life moves more slowly in villages. Many towns have only one store and one main road.

Quiet times on a farm (above) *and in the park* (above right)

Many city families take trips to the country to enjoy the peace and quiet.

Sharing Words

There are differences between the French language and the English language. But each has given words to the other. Some words are part English and part French, like *le sandwich,* *le weekend,* and *le fast food.* Can you figure out what these words mean?

This sign says hot and cold sandwiches are for sale. The French use English words for sandwiches and fast food.

The English language uses many words that come from the French language, like mayonnaise and casserole. But not all food words are the same in both languages. In France a cookie is called a *biscuit*.

Talking with Hands

French people use many hand signs to help them make their point when they are speaking. Here are some common ones.

Pointing to the cheek below your right eye: I don't believe it!

Rubbing your cheek with the back of your hand: It's boring!

Apartments rise high in the seaside city of Biarritz.

Houses hug the road in the Burgundy region.

Homes

What is a French home like? In the cities, many people live in apartments. The doorway to the building stands just a few feet from the busy street. Some old apartments are very small—only two or three rooms. Newer apartments give families more space. In villages rows of stone houses sometimes face the park at the center of town. Farmhouses in the country are bigger.

Old Homes

Some of the oldest homes in France are castles called *châteaus* (shah-TOHZ). The castles are built of stone and have tall towers, many rooms, and big gardens. Rich French people lived in the castles long ago to be safe from invaders.

The castle, or château, in the city of Angers was built more than 700 years ago!

Family

French families once were large. In some houses, children

Fixing a bike (above) *and enjoying a meal* (below)

All in the Family

Here are the French names for family members.

father	*père*	(PEHR)
mother	*mère*	(MEHR)
grandfather	*grand-père*	(grahn-PEHR)
grandmother	*grand-mère*	(grahn-MEHR)
uncle	*oncle*	(OHN-kluh)
aunt	*tante*	(TAHNT)
son	*fils*	(FEES)
daughter	*fille*	(FEE)
brother	*frère*	(FREHR)
sister	*sœur*	(SUR)

grew up with grandparents, aunts, and uncles all living under the same roof. But modern French families are smaller. Most parents have only one or two children.

Food

French people sometimes say *bon appétit* before they begin to eat a meal. They are wishing one another "good appetite!" in French.

All over France people enjoy long, thin, crunchy loaves of bread called baguettes. The French buy these loaves from bakeries. Sometimes the baguettes go with cheese. France makes

Mmm. Warm baguettes from the local bakery!

many cheeses—from smooth to stinky!

France also has many fine desserts. Poires Hélène is a simple dish of pears with ice cream and chocolate syrup. Yum!

France is famous for cheese (above) and for quiche (below).

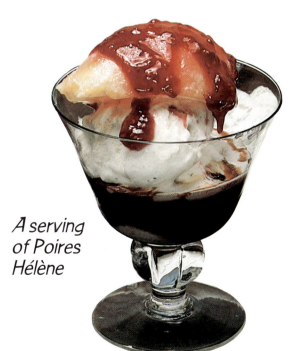

A serving of Poires Hélène

And More Food

(Above) *Fishers bring in the makings for a famous fish stew.*
(Below) *Thin pancakes, called crêpes, can be filled with meat, vegetables, or fruit.*

Each area of France prepares its own special food. The people in eastern France like to eat snails. Bretons, people who live in the northwest, often eat thin pancakes called crêpes. The apples grown in the north go into cider and pastries. In the south, on the Mediterranean coast, people eat a fish stew that uses seafood caught nearby.

New Foods

Have you ever eaten snails, frog legs, or sheep's brains? You might if you visited France!

Shopping

In France some shops sell just one kind of food. You might buy bread, meat, and cheese at three different stores. Many towns have a big outdoor market. Stalls line the sidewalks. Vegetable sellers sing about tomatoes and

In small French markets, the owner picks out your fruit or vegetables for you.

Jeans are on sale at this flea market in Paris.

potatoes. Laughter from the fish stall fills the air. People sometimes bring along their small dogs for the fun. They say *Waouf! Waouf!*

Some towns have a flea market where sellers spread all kinds of secondhand goods on tables or on the ground. Shoppers look for treasures.

A teacher helps a student with a math problem.

School and Summer

Do you want to visit a French school? Classes begin at eight or nine o'clock in the morning and go until four or five o'clock in the afternoon. Every night kids read and do their homework. Schools are closed on

After-school soccer games are popular.

with playgrounds, soccer fields, and places for indoor games and crafts.

Wednesdays. Students go to classes on Saturday mornings instead.

French kids don't goof off in the summer. Every town has a summer camp,

Kids in France have homework every night. Do you?

Faiths of France

Most people in France belong to the Roman Catholic Church. Smaller numbers of the French are members of the Islamic, Protestant, and Jewish faiths. Christmas and Easter are the most important Christian holidays in France. People crowd the churches on these days. A stone or brick Catholic

A Roman Catholic priest blesses the bride and groom.

church stands near the center of every French town. Some towns have very beautiful, tall churches called cathedrals. Stained-glass windows line the walls.

This stained-glass window is from a church in the city of Chartres.

Colored Glass

The walls of some large French churches hold colorful stained-glass windows. To make the windows, artists put together bits of colored glass.

Soldiers parade in the streets on Bastille Day. Even the French president gets involved!

Let's Celebrate!

It's July 14—Bastille Day! Crowds of people stand along the street for a parade. A band plays. Fireworks burst over the streets. Bastille Day is the French national holiday. On this day, the nation remembers a famous riot at a prison called the Bastille. Because of the riot, France stopped having a king.

The French also celebrate other holidays. Some of these holidays are only celebrated in one area, instead of all over France.

People wave colorful flags, called pennants, during a local festival in Lyons.

April Fish Day

On April 1, the French celebrate *Poisson d'avril* (pwah-SOHN dah-VREEL). That means "April Fish" in French. French kids cut a fish out of paper or cloth on this day. They try to sneak up and stick the fish on a friend's back. Then other kids point and shout "Poisson d'avril!"

Vacation

Almost everyone in France goes on vacation in August. Stores and factories close. The cities sure get quiet!

Many families head for the beach. Some families go to the country. Kids play soccer, tennis, or a game called *pétanque*. Some days they fish and swim in nearby rivers. In winter the French might go to the Alps to ski or sled.

Got one! A family fishes during its summer vacation.

Hi Mom! Hi Dad!

Granny and I went to see a long, long piece of cloth today. Granny says it is called a tapestry (she helped me spell it). And we are in the town of Bayeux (she helped me spell that word, too). So the cloth is called the Bayeux Tapestry. It has lots of little pictures that show kings and knights and fighting. I thought it was pretty cool.

Love,
Tommy

(Above left) *In winter some French people head for the snow-covered Alps.* (Left) *Pétanque players measure how far their large metal ball is from the smaller wooden ball.*

On Your Bikes!

Bikes whoosh by on narrow country lanes. Motor scooters rush after them. A lot of cars and vans follow the bikes. People stand along the roads clapping and yelling. What's all the fuss? The Tour de France!

The race is on for these cyclists in the Tour de France.

Every summer bike racers from all over the world come to France. They follow a long route around the country. The race lasts three weeks. Riders go over plains and mountains. Racers go through many towns, but the Tour de France always ends in Paris.

Story Time

French people of all ages love to read. Babar, Beauty and the Beast, and the Little Prince are famous characters from French books. Have you heard of *The Tales of Mother Goose?* Some of the book's stories are "Puss in Boots," "Sleeping Beauty," "Little Red Riding Hood," and "Cinderella." A French author

named Charles Perrault wrote these tales long ago.

The French think highly of their writers. They may be chosen to be a member of the French Academy—the French writers' Hall of Fame.

Storytelling

Tell someone a story about France. You can pretend you live in France or are visiting a French friend. What would you do? Would you ride in the Tour de France? Would you explore the castles along the Loire River? Would you ski down the Alps?

A famous painting in the Louvre called the Mona Lisa *(above) and a* Lascaux cave painting *(below)*

Art

One way to get really tired feet in France is to go to the Louvre. This huge palace was turned into an art museum. The Louvre holds more than a million paintings, drawings, sculptures, pieces of jewelry, and other objects. It is

Painting with a Point

A Frenchman named Georges Seurat made up a new way to paint pictures. He put a dab of paint on the point of his brush. Then he placed the dabs close to one another to make a shape. You could only see the shape by stepping away from the painting.

fun to walk through the glass **pyramid** to enter the museum.

Not all art in France is in museums. One day four French boys were looking for their dog. One boy fell into a cave. He looked around. On the walls were old pictures of a bull, horses, and animals like buffalo. Wow! The boys had found the Lascaux Caves.

The Bayeux Tapestry is a long, long, long piece of cloth. It shows people and events that happened in France a long, long, long time ago.

New Words to Learn

canal: A waterway made by humans to link rivers to one another.

capital: A city where the government is located.

continent: Any one of seven large areas of land. The continents are Africa, Antarctica, Asia, Australia, Europe, North America, and South America.

map: A drawing or chart of all or part of the earth or sky.

mountain: A part of the earth's surface that rises high into the sky.

plateau: An area of high, level land.

pyramid: A structure with a square (four equal sides) floor and four triangular walls. The three-sided walls start out wide near the ground and get narrower until they come to a point at the top.

The three-part French flag is called the tricolor, meaning three colors.

New Words to Say

Arc de Triomphe	AHRK duh tree-OHNF
Bayeux	bay-YOO
chien	SHYAN
Lascaux	lah-SKOH
Loire	LWAHR
Louvre	LOO-vruh
Massif Central	mah-SEEF sahn-TRAHL
Poires Hélène	PWAHR ay-LEHN
pétanque	pay-TAHNK
Pyrénées	peer-uh-NEEZ
Seine	SEHN
Versailles	vehr-SY

More Books to Read

Aliki. *The King's Day.* New York: Thomas Y. Crowell, 1989.

Chrisp, Peter. *The Normans.* New York: Thomson Learning, 1995.

Haskins, Jim and Kathleen Benson. *Count Your Way through France.* Minneapolis: Carolrhoda Books, Inc., 1996.

Haviland, Virginia. *Favorite Fairy Tales Told in France,* retold from Charles Perrault and Others. New York: Beech Tree Books, 1994.

Montaufier, Poupa. *One Summer at Grandmother's House.* Minneapolis: Carolrhoda Books, Inc., 1983.

Munroe, Roxie. *The Inside-Outside Book of Paris.* New York: Dutton Children's Books, 1992.

Regan, Mary. *A Family in France.* Minneapolis: Lerner Publications Company, 1985.

Sturges, Jo. *Discovering France.* New York: Crestwood House, 1993.

New Words to Find

art, 42–43

Bastille Day, 34

canals, 7, 10
castles, 21
cities, 8–9, 11, 16–17

families, 22–23
food, 24–25, 26–27

games, 31, 36

holidays, 32, 34–35
houses, 20–21

languages, 15, 18–19, 23
Lascaux Caves, 43
Loire River, 7
Louvre, 42–43

map of France, 4–5

markets, 28–29
Massif Central, 6
mountains, 6

Paris, 8–9, 39
people, 12–13, 14–15

religion, 32–33

schools, 30–31
Seine River, 8
sports, 38–39
storytelling, 40–41

Tour de France, 38–39
towns, 10, 17
travel methods, 7, 10–11, 16

vacations, 36–37

```
CRC     Streissguth, Thomas,
TB      France /
944
.081
STR
```